HERSHEY'S®

BROWNIES AND MORE™

D1059280

Cookie Jar Favorites

Who can resist the aroma of fresh-baked cookies wafting through the house? Whatever recipe you choose, you're sure to please family and friends with these chocolate-filled delights.

Chocolate Chips and Raspberry Bars

1 1/2 cups all-purpose flour
1/2 cup sugar
1/2 teaspoon baking powder
1/2 teaspoon salt
1/2 cup (1 stick) butter or margarine, softened
1 egg, beaten
1/4 cup milk
1/4 teaspoon vanilla extract
3/4 cup raspberry preserves
1 cup HERSHEY'S Semi-Sweet Chocolate Chips

1. Heat oven to 400°F. Grease 13×9×2-inch baking pan.

2. Stir together flour, sugar, baking powder and salt in large bowl. Cut in butter with pastry blender or two knives until mixture resembles coarse crumbs. Add egg, milk and vanilla; beat on medium speed of mixer until well blended.

3. Reserve 1/2 cup mixture for topping. Spread remaining mixture onto bottom of prepared pan (this will be a very thin layer). Spread preserves evenly over batter; sprinkle chocolate chips over top. Drop reserved batter by 1/2 teaspoons over chips.

4. Bake 25 minutes or until golden. Cool completely in pan on wire rack. Cut into bars.   *Makes about 32 bars*

Tip: Rich, buttery bar cookies and brownies freeze extremely well. Freeze in airtight containers or freezer bags for up to three months. Thaw at room temperature.

3

Hershey's "Perfectly Chocolate" Chocolate Chip Cookies

2$\frac{1}{4}$ cups all-purpose flour
$\frac{1}{3}$ cup HERSHEY'S Cocoa
1 teaspoon baking soda
$\frac{1}{2}$ teaspoon salt
1 cup (2 sticks) butter or margarine, softened
$\frac{3}{4}$ cup granulated sugar
$\frac{3}{4}$ cup packed light brown sugar
1 teaspoon vanilla extract
2 eggs
2 cups (12-ounce package) HERSHEY'S Semi-Sweet
   Chocolate Chips
1 cup chopped nuts (optional)

1. Heat oven to 375°F.

2. Stir together flour, cocoa, baking soda and salt. Beat butter, granulated sugar, brown sugar and vanilla in large bowl on medium speed of mixer until creamy. Add eggs; beat well. Gradually add flour mixture, beating until well blended. Stir in chocolate chips and nuts, if desired. Drop by rounded teaspoons onto ungreased cookie sheet.

3. Bake 8 to 10 minutes or until set. Cool slightly; remove from cookie sheet to wire rack.   *Makes about 5 dozen cookies*

Hershey's "Perfectly Chocolate" Chocolate Chip Cookies

Five Layer Bars

   ³/₄ cup (1¹/₂ sticks) butter or margarine
1³/₄ cups graham cracker crumbs
   ¹/₄ cup HERSHEY'S Cocoa
   2 tablespoons sugar
   1 can (14 ounces) sweetened condensed milk (not evaporated milk)
   1 cup HERSHEY'S Semi-Sweet Chocolate Chips
   1 cup raisins, chopped dried apricots or miniature marshmallows
   1 cup chopped nuts

1. Heat oven to 350°F. Place butter in 13×9×2-inch baking pan. Heat in oven until melted. Remove pan from oven.

2. Stir together graham cracker crumbs, cocoa and sugar; sprinkle evenly over butter. Pour sweetened condensed milk evenly over crumb mixture. Sprinkle with chocolate chips and raisins. Sprinkle nuts on top; press down firmly.

3. Bake 25 to 30 minutes or until lightly browned. Cool completely in pan on wire rack. Cover with foil; let stand at room temperature 6 to 8 hours. Cut into bars.   *Makes about 36 bars*

Variation: Substitute 1 cup REESE'S Peanut Butter Chips for chocolate chips. Sprinkle 1 cup golden raisins or chopped dried apricots over chips. Proceed as above.

Cocoa Kiss Cookies

    1 cup (2 sticks) butter or margarine, softened
    $^2/_3$ cup sugar
    1 teaspoon vanilla extract
 1$^2/_3$ cups all-purpose flour
    $^1/_4$ cup HERSHEY'S Cocoa
    1 cup finely chopped pecans
        About 54 HERSHEY'S KISSES Milk Chocolates
        Powdered sugar

1. Beat butter, sugar and vanilla in large bowl until creamy. Stir together flour and cocoa; gradually add to butter mixture, beating until well blended. Add pecans; beat until well blended. Refrigerate dough about 1 hour or until firm enough to handle.

2. Heat oven to 375°F. Remove wrappers from chocolate pieces. Mold scant tablespoon of dough around each chocolate piece, covering completely. Shape into balls. Place on ungreased cookie sheet.

3. Bake 10 to 12 minutes or until set. Cool about 1 minute; remove from cookie sheet to wire rack. Cool completely. Roll in powdered sugar. Roll in sugar again just before serving, if desired.

Makes about 4$^1/_2$ dozen cookies

Hershey's Classic Chocolate Chip Cookies

1 cup (2 sticks) butter, softened
¾ cup granulated sugar
¾ cup packed light brown sugar
1 teaspoon vanilla extract
2 eggs
2¼ cups all-purpose flour
1 teaspoon baking soda
½ teaspoon salt
2 cups (12-ounce package) HERSHEY'S Semi-Sweet
  Chocolate Chips
1 cup chopped nuts (optional)

1. Heat oven to 375°F.

2. Beat butter, granulated sugar, brown sugar and vanilla in large bowl until creamy. Add eggs; beat well. Stir together flour, baking soda and salt; gradually add to butter mixture, beating well. Stir in chocolate chips and nuts, if desired. Drop dough by rounded teaspoons onto ungreased cookie sheet.

3. Bake 8 to 10 minutes or until lightly browned. Cool slightly; remove from cookie sheet to wire rack. Cool completely.

Makes about 6 dozen cookies

Pan recipe: Spread dough into greased 15½×10½×1-inch jelly-roll pan. Bake at 375°F for 20 minutes or until lightly browned. Cool completely in pan on wire rack. Cut into bars. Makes about 48 bars.

Skor & Chocolate Chip Cookies: Omit 1 cup HERSHEY'S Semi-Sweet Chocolate Chips and nuts; replace with 1 cup finely chopped SKOR bars. Drop onto cookie sheets and bake as directed.

Ice Cream Sandwiches: Prepare cookies as directed. Place one small scoop slightly softened vanilla ice cream between flat sides of two cookies. Gently press together. Wrap and freeze.

Top to bottom: Cocoa Kiss Cookies (page 7), Hershey's Classic Chocolate Chip Cookies

Rich Chocolate Chip Toffee Bars

2$\frac{1}{3}$ cups all-purpose flour
$\frac{2}{3}$ cup packed light brown sugar
$\frac{3}{4}$ cup (1$\frac{1}{2}$ sticks) butter or margarine
1 egg, slightly beaten
2 cups (12-ounce package) HERSHEY'S Semi-Sweet
    Chocolate Chips, divided
1 cup coarsely chopped nuts
1 can (14 ounces) sweetened condensed milk (not evaporated
    milk)
1$\frac{3}{4}$ cups (10-ounce package) SKOR English Toffee Bits, divided

1. Heat oven to 350°F. Grease 13×9×2-inch baking pan.

2. Stir together flour and brown sugar in large bowl. Cut in butter with pastry blender until mixture resembles coarse crumbs. Add egg; mix well. Stir in 1$\frac{1}{2}$ cups chocolate chips and nuts. Reserve 1$\frac{1}{2}$ cups mixture. Press remaining crumb mixture onto bottom of prepared pan.

3. Bake 10 minutes. Pour sweetened condensed milk evenly over hot crust. Top with 1$\frac{1}{2}$ cups toffee bits. Sprinkle reserved crumb mixture and remaining $\frac{1}{2}$ cup chips over top.

4. Bake 25 to 30 minutes or until golden brown. Sprinkle with remaining $\frac{1}{4}$ cup toffee bits. Cool completely in pan on wire rack. Cut into bars. *Makes about 36 bars*

Rich Chocolate Chip Toffee Bars

Fudgey German Chocolate Sandwich Cookies

1¾ cups all-purpose flour
1½ cups sugar
¾ cup (1½ sticks) butter or margarine, softened
⅔ cup HERSHEY'S Cocoa or HERSHEY'S Dutch Processed
    Cocoa
¾ teaspoon baking soda
¼ teaspoon salt
2 eggs
2 tablespoons milk
1 teaspoon vanilla extract
½ cup finely chopped pecans
    Coconut and Pecan Filling (recipe follows)

1. Heat oven to 350°F.

2. Combine flour, sugar, butter, cocoa, baking soda, salt, eggs, milk and vanilla in large bowl. Beat at medium speed of mixer until blended (batter will be stiff). Stir in pecans.

3. Form dough into 1¼-inch balls. Place on ungreased cookie sheet; flatten slightly.

4. Bake 9 to 11 minutes or until almost set. Cool slightly; remove from cookie sheet to wire rack. Cool completely. Spread about 1 heaping tablespoon Coconut and Pecan Filling onto bottom of one cookie. Top with second cookie to make sandwich. Serve warm or at room temperature.   *Makes about 17 sandwich cookies*

Prep Time: 25 minutes
Bake Time: 9 minutes
Cool Time: 35 minutes

Coconut and Pecan Filling

$^1/_2$ cup (1 stick) butter or margarine
$^1/_2$ cup packed light brown sugar
$^1/_4$ cup light corn syrup
1 cup MOUNDS Sweetened Coconut Flakes, toasted*
1 cup finely chopped pecans
1 teaspoon vanilla extract

*To toast coconut: Heat oven to 350°F. Spread coconut in even layer on baking sheet. Bake 6 to 8 minutes, stirring occasionally, until golden.

Melt butter in medium saucepan over medium heat; add brown sugar and corn syrup. Stir constantly, until thick and bubbly. Remove from heat; stir in coconut, pecans and vanilla. Use warm.

Makes about 2 cups filling

Fudgey German Chocolate Sandwich Cookies

13

Peanut Butter Chip Triangles

 1½ cups all-purpose flour
 ½ cup packed light brown sugar
 ½ cup (1 stick) cold butter or margarine
 1⅔ cups (10-ounce package) REESE'S Peanut Butter Chips,
 divided
 1 can (14 ounces) sweetened condensed milk (not evaporated
 milk)
 1 egg, slightly beaten
 1 teaspoon vanilla extract
 ¾ cup chopped walnuts
 Powdered sugar (optional)

1. Heat oven to 350°F. Stir together flour and brown sugar in medium bowl. Cut in butter with pastry blender or fork until mixture resembles coarse crumbs. Stir in ½ cup peanut butter chips. Press mixture into bottom of ungreased 13×9×2-inch baking pan. Bake 15 minutes.

2. Meanwhile, combine sweetened condensed milk, egg and vanilla in large bowl. Stir in remaining chips and walnuts. Spread evenly over hot baked crust.

3. Bake 25 minutes or until golden brown. Cool completely in pan on wire rack. Cut into 2- or 2½-inch squares; cut squares diagonally into triangles. Sift powdered sugar over top, if desired.

Makes 24 or 40 triangles

Tip: To sprinkle powdered sugar over brownies, bars, cupcakes or other desserts, place sugar in a wire mesh strainer. Hold over top of desserts and gently tap sides of strainer.

Prep Time: 20 minutes
Bake Time: 40 minutes
Cool Time: 2 hours

Peanut Butter Chip Triangles

Oatmeal Butterscotch Cookies

$3/4$ cup ($1^1/2$ sticks) butter or margarine, softened
$3/4$ cup granulated sugar
$3/4$ cup packed light brown sugar
2 eggs
1 teaspoon vanilla extract
$1^1/4$ cups all-purpose flour
1 teaspoon baking soda
$1/2$ teaspoon salt
$1/2$ teaspoon ground cinnamon
3 cups quick-cooking or regular rolled oats, uncooked
$1^2/3$ cups (10-ounce package) HERSHEY'S Butterscotch Chips

1. Heat oven to 375°F.

2. Beat butter, granulated sugar and brown sugar in large bowl until well blended. Add eggs and vanilla; blend thoroughly. Stir together flour, baking soda, salt and cinnamon; gradually add to butter mixture, beating until well blended. Stir in oats and butterscotch chips; mix well. Drop by teaspoons onto ungreased cookie sheet.

3. Bake 8 to 10 minutes or until golden brown. Cool slightly; remove from cookie sheet to wire rack. Cool completely.

Makes about 4 dozen cookies

Oatmeal Butterscotch Cookies

Almond Fudge Topped Shortbread

1 cup (2 sticks) butter or margarine, softened
$1/2$ cup powdered sugar
$1/4$ teaspoon salt
$1^1/4$ cups all-purpose flour
2 cups (12-ounce package) HERSHEY'S Semi-Sweet
    Chocolate Chips
1 (14-ounce) can sweetened condensed milk (not evaporated
    milk)
$1/2$ teaspoon almond extract
$1/2$ cup sliced almonds, toasted

1. Heat oven to 350°F. Grease 13×9×2-inch baking pan.

2. Beat butter, powdered sugar and salt in large bowl until fluffy. Add flour; mix well. With floured hands, press evenly into prepared pan.

3. Bake 20 minutes or until lightly browned.

4. Melt chocolate chips and sweetened condensed milk in heavy saucepan over low heat, stirring constantly. Remove from heat; stir in extract. Spread evenly over baked shortbread. Garnish with almonds; press down firmly. Cool. Chill 3 hours or until firm. Cut into bars. Store covered at room temperature.   *Makes 24 to 36 bars*

Almond Fudge Topped Shortbread

Peanut Butter and Chocolate Cookie Sandwich Cookies

$^1/_2$ cup REESE'S Peanut Butter Chips
3 tablespoons plus $^1/_2$ cup (1 stick) butter or margarine, softened and divided
1$^1/_4$ cups sugar, divided
$^1/_4$ cup light corn syrup
1 egg
1 teaspoon vanilla extract
2 cups plus 2 tablespoons all-purpose flour, divided
2 teaspoons baking soda
$^1/_4$ teaspoon salt
$^1/_2$ cup HERSHEY'S Cocoa
5 tablespoons butter or margarine, melted
Additional sugar
About 2 dozen large marshmallows

1. Heat oven to 350°F. Melt peanut butter chips and 3 tablespoons softened butter in small saucepan over very low heat. Remove from heat; cool slightly.

2. Beat remaining $^1/_2$ cup softened butter and 1 cup sugar in large bowl until fluffy. Add corn syrup, egg and vanilla; blend thoroughly. Stir together 2 cups flour, baking soda and salt; add to butter mixture, blending well. Remove 1$^1/_4$ cups batter and place in small bowl; with wooden spoon, stir in remaining 2 tablespoons flour and melted peanut butter chip mixture.

3. Blend cocoa, remaining $^1/_4$ cup sugar and 5 tablespoons melted butter into remaining batter. Refrigerate both doughs 5 to 10 minutes or until firm enough to handle. Shape each dough into 1-inch balls; roll in sugar. Place on ungreased cookie sheet.

4. Bake 10 to 11 minutes or until set. Cool slightly; remove from cookie sheet to wire racks. Cool completely. Place 1 marshmallow on flat side of 1 chocolate cookie. Microwave at MEDIUM (50% power) 10 seconds or until marshmallow is softened. Place a peanut butter cookie over marshmallow; press down lightly. Repeat for remaining cookies. Serve immediately.

Makes about 2 dozen sandwich cookies

Peanut Butter and Chocolate Cookie Sandwich Cookies

21

Three-in-One Chocolate Chip Cookies

6 tablespoons butter or margarine, softened
$^1/_2$ cup packed light brown sugar
$^1/_4$ cup granulated sugar
1 egg
1 teaspoon vanilla extract
1$^1/_2$ cups all-purpose flour
$^1/_2$ teaspoon baking soda
$^1/_4$ teaspoon salt
2 cups (12-ounce package) HERSHEY'S Semi-Sweet
    Chocolate Chips

Beat butter, brown sugar and granulated sugar in large bowl until fluffy. Add egg and vanilla; beat well. Stir together flour, baking soda and salt; gradually blend into butter mixture. Stir in chocolate chips. Shape and bake cookies into one of the three versions below.

Giant Cookie: Prepare dough. Heat oven to 350°F. Line 12×$^5/_8$-inch round pizza pan with foil. Pat dough evenly into prepared pan to within $^3/_4$ inch of edge. Bake 15 to 18 minutes or until lightly browned. Cool completely; cut into wedges. Decorate or garnish as desired. Makes about 8 servings (one 12-inch cookie).

Medium-Size Refrigerator Cookies: Prepare dough. On wax paper, shape into 2 rolls, 1$^1/_2$ inches in diameter. Wrap in wax paper; cover with plastic wrap. Refrigerate several hours, or until firm enough to slice. Heat oven to 350°F. Remove rolls from refrigerator; remove wrapping. With sharp knife, cut into $^1/_4$-inch-wide slices. Place on ungreased cookie sheet, about 3 inches apart. Bake 8 to 10 minutes or until lightly browned. Cool slightly; remove from cookie sheet to wire rack. Cool completely. Makes about 2$^1/_2$ dozen (2$^1/_2$-inch) cookies.

Miniature Cookies: Prepare dough. Heat oven to 350°F. Drop dough by $\frac{1}{4}$ teaspoons onto ungreased cookie sheet, about $1\frac{1}{2}$ inches apart. (Or, spoon dough into disposable plastic frosting bag; cut about $\frac{1}{4}$ inch off tip. Squeeze batter by $\frac{1}{4}$ teaspoons onto ungreased cookie sheet.) Bake 5 to 7 minutes or just until set. Cool slightly; remove from cookie sheet to wire rack. Cool completely. Makes about $18\frac{1}{2}$ dozen ($\frac{3}{4}$-inch) cookies.

Three-in-One Chocolate Chip Cookies

Irresistible Brownies

Fudgey, rich, chunky, chewy brownies are a true chocolate lover's dream. Drizzled with caramel, studded with chips, covered with frosting . . . . mmmmm.

Hershey's White Chip Brownies

    4 eggs
1 1/4 cups sugar
  1/2 cup (1 stick) butter or margarine, melted
    2 teaspoons vanilla extract
1 1/3 cups all-purpose flour
  2/3 cup HERSHEY'S Cocoa
    1 teaspoon baking powder
  1/2 teaspoon salt
1 2/3 cups (10-ounce package) HERSHEY'S Premier White
      Chips

1. Heat oven to 350°F. Grease 13×9×2-inch baking pan.

2. Beat eggs in large bowl until foamy; gradually beat in sugar. Add butter and vanilla; beat until blended. Stir together flour, cocoa, baking powder and salt; add to egg mixture, beating until blended. Stir in white chips. Spread batter into prepared pan.

3. Bake 25 to 30 minutes or until brownies begin to pull away from sides of pan. Cool completely in pan on wire rack. Cut into squares.

Makes about 36 brownies

Tip: Brownies and bar cookies cut into different shapes can add interest to a plate of simple square cookies. Cut cookies into different size rectangles or make triangles by cutting them into 2- to 2 1/2-inch squares; cut each square in half diagonally. To make diamond shapes, cut straight lines 1 or 1 1/2 inches apart the length of the baking pan, then cut straight lines 1 1/2 inches apart diagonally across the pan.

Prep Time: 15 minutes
Bake Time: 25 minutes
Cool Time: 2 hours

P.B. Chips Brownie Cups

1 cup (2 sticks) butter or margarine
2 cups sugar
2 teaspoons vanilla extract
4 eggs
3/4 cup HERSHEY'S Cocoa or HERSHEY'S Dutch Processed
Cocoa
1 3/4 cups all-purpose flour
1/2 teaspoon baking powder
1/2 teaspoon salt
1 2/3 cups (10-ounce package) REESE'S Peanut Butter Chips,
divided

1. Heat oven to 350°F. Line 18 muffin cups (2 1/2 inches in diameter) with paper or foil bake cups.

2. Place butter in large microwave-safe bowl. Microwave at HIGH (100%) 1 to 1 1/2 minutes or until melted. Stir in sugar and vanilla. Add eggs; beat well. Add cocoa; beat until well blended. Add flour, baking powder and salt; beat well. Stir in 1 1/3 cups peanut butter chips. Divide batter evenly into muffin cups.

3. Bake 25 to 30 minutes or until surface is firm; remove from oven. Immediately sprinkle remaining 1/3 cup peanut butter chips over muffin tops, pressing in slightly. Cool completely in pan on wire rack.

Makes about 1 1/2 dozen brownie cups

P.B. Chips Brownie Cups

Brownie Pie à la Mode

$^1/_2$ cup sugar
2 tablespoons butter or margarine
2 tablespoons water
1$^1/_3$ cups HERSHEY'S Semi-Sweet Chocolate Chips
2 eggs
$^2/_3$ cup all-purpose flour
$^1/_4$ teaspoon baking soda
$^1/_4$ teaspoon salt
1 teaspoon vanilla extract
$^3/_4$ cup chopped nuts (optional)
Fudge Sauce (recipe follows, optional)
Ice cream, any flavor

1. Heat oven to 350°F. Grease 9-inch pie plate.

2. Combine sugar, butter and water in medium saucepan. Cook over medium heat, stirring occasionally, just until mixture comes to a boil. Remove from heat. Immediately add chocolate chips; stir until melted. Add eggs; beat with spoon until well blended.

3. Stir together flour, baking soda and salt. Add to chocolate mixture; stir until well blended. Stir in vanilla and nuts, if desired; pour into prepared pie plate.

4. Bake 25 to 30 minutes or until almost set. (Pie will not test done in center.) Cool. Prepare Fudge Sauce, if desired. Top pie with scoops of ice cream and prepared sauce. *Makes 8 to 10 servings*

Fudge Sauce

1 cup HERSHEY'S Semi-Sweet Chocolate Chips
$^1/_2$ cup evaporated milk
$^1/_4$ cup sugar
1 tablespoon butter or margarine

Combine all ingredients in medium microwave-safe bowl. Microwave at HIGH (100%) 1 minute; stir. If necessary, microwave at HIGH an additional 15 seconds at a time, stirring after each heating, just until chips are melted and mixture is smooth. Cool slightly.

Makes about 1$^1/_2$ cups sauce

Brownie Pie à la Mode

29

Quick & Easy Fudgey Brownies

4 bars (1 ounce each) HERSHEY'S Unsweetened Baking Chocolate, broken into pieces
³/₄ cup (1¹/₂ sticks) butter or margarine
2 cups sugar
3 eggs
1¹/₂ teaspoons vanilla extract
1 cup all-purpose flour
1 cup chopped nuts (optional)
Creamy Quick Chocolate Frosting (recipe follows, optional)

1. Heat oven to 350°F. Grease 13×9×2-inch baking pan.

2. Place chocolate and butter in large microwave-safe bowl. Microwave at HIGH (100%) 1¹/₂ to 2 minutes or until chocolate is melted and mixture is smooth when stirred. Add sugar; stir with spoon until well blended. Add eggs and vanilla; mix well. Add flour and nuts, if desired; stir until well blended. Spread into prepared pan.

3. Bake 30 to 35 minutes or until wooden pick inserted in center comes out almost clean. Cool in pan on wire rack.

4. Frost with Creamy Quick Chocolate Frosting, if desired. Cut into squares. *Makes about 24 brownies*

Creamy Quick Chocolate Frosting

   3 tablespoons butter or margarine
   3 bars (1 ounce each) HERSHEY'S Unsweetened Baking
      Chocolate, broken into pieces
   3 cups powdered sugar
   1/2 cup milk
   1 teaspoon vanilla extract
   1/8 teaspoon salt

Melt butter and chocolate in saucepan over very low heat. Cook, stirring constantly, until chocolate is melted and mixture is smooth. Pour into large bowl; add powdered sugar, milk, vanilla and salt. Beat on medium speed of mixer until well blended. If necessary, refrigerate 10 minutes or until of spreading consistency.

Makes about 2 cups frosting

Quick & Easy Fudgey Brownies

Three Great Tastes Blond Brownies

2 cups packed light brown sugar
1 cup (2 sticks) butter or margarine, melted
2 eggs
2 teaspoons vanilla extract
2 cups all-purpose flour
1 teaspoon salt
$^2/_3$ cup (of each) HERSHEY'S Semi-Sweet Chocolate Chips,
     REESE'S Peanut Butter Chips, and HERSHEY'S
     Premier White Chips
Chocolate Chip Drizzle (recipe follows)

1. Heat oven to 350°F. Grease $15^1/_2 \times 10^1/_2 \times 1$-inch jelly-roll pan.

2. Stir together brown sugar and butter in large bowl; beat in eggs and vanilla until smooth. Add flour and salt, beating just until blended; stir in chocolate, peanut butter and white chips. Spread batter into prepared pan.

3. Bake 25 to 30 minutes or until wooden pick inserted in center comes out clean. Cool completely in pan on wire rack. Cut into bars. With tines of fork, drizzle Chocolate Chip Drizzle over bars.

Makes about 72 bars

Chocolate Chip Drizzle: Place $^1/_4$ cup HERSHEY'S Semi-Sweet Chocolate Chips and $^1/_4$ teaspoon shortening (do not use butter, margarine, spread or oil) in small microwave-safe bowl. Microwave at HIGH (100%) 30 seconds to 1 minute; stir until chips are melted and mixture is smooth.

Three Great Tastes Blond Brownies

Brownie Caramel Pecan Bars

$^1/_2$ cup sugar
2 tablespoons butter or margarine
2 tablespoons water
2 cups (12-ounce package) HERSHEY'S Semi-Sweet
    Chocolate Chips, divided
2 eggs
1 teaspoon vanilla extract
$^2/_3$ cup all-purpose flour
$^1/_4$ teaspoon baking soda
$^1/_4$ teaspoon salt
    Classic Caramel Topping (recipe follows)
1 cup pecan pieces

1. Heat oven to 350°F. Line 9-inch square baking pan with foil, extending foil over edges of pan. Grease and flour foil.

2. Combine sugar, butter and water in medium saucepan. Cook over low heat, stirring constantly, until mixture boils. Remove from heat. Immediately add 1 cup chocolate chips; stir until melted. Beat in eggs and vanilla until well blended. Stir together flour, baking soda and salt; stir into chocolate mixture. Spread batter into prepared pan.

3. Bake 15 to 20 minutes or until brownies begin to pull away from sides of pan. Meanwhile, prepare Classic Caramel Topping. Remove brownies from oven; immediately and carefully spread with prepared topping. Sprinkle remaining 1 cup chips and pecans over topping. Cool completely in pan on wire rack, being careful not to disturb chips while soft. Lift out of pan. Cut into bars.   *Makes about 16 bars*

Classic Caramel Topping: Remove wrappers from 25 HERSHEY'S Classic Caramels. Combine ¼ cup (½ stick) butter or margarine, caramels and 2 tablespoons milk in medium microwave-safe bowl. Microwave at HIGH (100%) 1 minute; stir. Microwave an additional 1 to 2 minutes, stirring every 30 seconds, or until caramels are melted and mixture is smooth when stirred. Use immediately.

Brownie Caramel Pecan Bars

Miniature Brownie Cups

6 tablespoons butter or margarine, melted
$^3/_4$ cup sugar
$^1/_2$ teaspoon vanilla extract
2 eggs
$^1/_2$ cup all-purpose flour
$^1/_4$ cup HERSHEY'S Cocoa or HERSHEY'S Dutch Processed
    Cocoa
$^1/_4$ teaspoon baking powder
    Dash salt
$^1/_4$ cup finely chopped nuts

1. Heat oven to 350°F. Line small muffin cups ($1^3/_4$ inches in diameter) with paper bake cups. Stir together butter, sugar and vanilla in medium bowl. Add eggs; beat well with spoon.

2. Stir together flour, cocoa, baking powder and salt; gradually add to butter mixture, beating with spoon until well blended. Fill muffin cups $^1/_2$ full with batter; sprinkle nuts over top.

3. Bake 12 to 15 minutes or until wooden pick inserted in center comes out almost clean. Cool slightly; remove brownies from pan to wire rack. Cool completely.   *Makes about 24 brownies*

Tip: HERSHEY'S Dutch Processed Cocoa involves a process which neutralizes the natural acidity found in cocoa powder. This results in a darker cocoa with a more mellow flavor than natural cocoa.

Prep Time: 20 minutes
Bake Time: 12 minutes
Cool Time: 25 minutes

Miniature Brownie Cups

Collectible Cakes & More

Here are the tried-and-true classics from the Hershey Kitchens—beautiful to look at and even better to eat. Layer cakes, cheesecakes, tortes and pies make unforgettable endings to any meal.

Classic Boston Cream Pie

$1/3$ cup shortening
1 cup sugar
2 eggs
1 teaspoon vanilla extract
$1^{1}/4$ cups all-purpose flour
$1^{1}/2$ teaspoons baking powder
$1/4$ teaspoon salt
$3/4$ cup milk
    Rich Filling (recipe page 40)
    Dark Cocoa Glaze (recipe page 40)

1. Heat oven to 350°F. Grease and flour 9-inch round baking pan.

2. Beat shortening, sugar, eggs and vanilla in large bowl until fluffy. Stir together flour, baking powder and salt; add alternately with milk to shortening mixture, beating well after each addition. Pour batter into prepared pan.

3. Bake 30 to 35 minutes or until wooden pick inserted in center comes out clean. Cool 10 minutes; remove from pan to wire rack. Cool completely.

4. Prepare Rich Filling. With long serrated knife, cut cake in half horizontally. Place one layer, cut side up, on serving plate; spread with prepared filling. Top with remaining layer, cut side down. Prepare Dark Cocoa Glaze; spread over cake, allowing glaze to run down sides. Refrigerate several hours or until cold. Garnish as desired. Refrigerate leftover pie. *Makes 8 to 10 servings*

continued on page 40

Classic Boston Cream Pie, continued

Dark Cocoa Glaze

> 3 tablespoons water
> 2 tablespoons butter or margarine
> 3 tablespoons HERSHEY'S Cocoa
> 1 cup powdered sugar
> 1/2 teaspoon vanilla extract

Heat water and butter in small saucepan over medium heat until mixture comes to a boil; remove from heat. Immediately stir in cocoa. Gradually add powdered sugar and vanilla, beating with whisk until smooth and of desired consistency; cool slightly.

Makes about 3/4 cup glaze

Rich Filling

> 1/3 cup sugar
> 2 tablespoons cornstarch
> 1 1/2 cups milk
> 2 egg yolks, slightly beaten
> 1 tablespoon butter or margarine
> 1 teaspoon vanilla extract

Stir together sugar and cornstarch in medium saucepan; gradually add milk and egg yolks, stirring until blended. Cook over medium heat, stirring constantly, until mixture comes to a boil. Boil 1 minute, stirring constantly. Remove from heat; stir in butter and vanilla. Cover; refrigerate several hours or until cold.

Makes about 1 3/4 cups filling

Chocolate Chip Walnut Pie

$^3/_4$ cup packed light brown sugar
$^1/_2$ cup all-purpose flour
$^1/_2$ teaspoon baking powder
$^1/_4$ teaspoon ground cinnamon
2 eggs, slightly beaten
1 cup HERSHEY'S MINI CHIPS™ Semi-Sweet Chocolate
    Chips, HERSHEY'S Semi-Sweet or Milk Chocolate
    Chips
1 cup coarsely chopped walnuts
1 baked (9-inch) pie crust
    Spiced Cream (recipe follows)

1. Heat oven to 350°F.

2. Combine brown sugar, flour, baking powder and cinnamon in medium bowl. Add eggs; stir until well blended. Add chocolate chips and walnuts. Pour into baked pie crust.

3. Bake 25 to 30 minutes or until lightly browned and set. Serve slightly warm or at room temperature with Spiced Cream. Refrigerate leftovers. *Makes 1 (9-inch) pie*

Spiced Cream: Combine $^1/_2$ cup chilled whipping cream, 1 tablespoon powdered sugar, $^1/_4$ teaspoon vanilla extract, $^1/_4$ teaspoon ground cinnamon and dash ground nutmeg in small bowl; beat until stiff. Makes about 1 cup topping.

Crunchy-Topped Cocoa Cake

1 1/2 cups all-purpose flour
1 cup sugar
1/4 cup HERSHEY'S Cocoa
1 teaspoon baking soda
1/2 teaspoon salt
1 cup water
1/4 cup plus 2 tablespoons vegetable oil
1 tablespoon white vinegar
1 teaspoon vanilla extract
Broiled Topping (recipe follows)

1. Heat oven to 350°F. Grease and flour 8-inch square baking pan.

2. Stir together flour, sugar, cocoa, baking soda and salt in large bowl. Add water, oil, vinegar and vanilla; beat with spoon or whisk just until batter is smooth and ingredients are well blended. Pour batter into prepared pan.

3. Bake 35 to 40 minutes or until wooden pick inserted in center comes out clean. Meanwhile, prepare Broiled Topping; spread on warm cake. Set oven to broil; place pan about 4 inches from heat. Broil 3 minutes or until top is bubbly and golden brown. Remove from oven. Cool completely in pan on wire rack.   *Makes 9 servings*

Prep Time: 20 minutes
Bake Time: 35 minutes
Cool Time: 1 1/2 hours

Broiled Topping

   $^1/_4$ cup ($^1/_2$ stick) butter or margarine, softened
   $^1/_2$ cup packed light brown sugar
   $^1/_2$ cup coarsely chopped nuts
   $^1/_2$ cup MOUNDS Sweetened Coconut Flakes
   3 tablespoons light cream or evaporated milk

Stir together all ingredients in small bowl until well blended.

Makes about 1 cup topping

Crunchy-Topped Cocoa Cake

Chilled Raspberry Cheesecake

1 1/2 cups vanilla wafer crumbs (about 45 wafers, crushed)
1/3 cup HERSHEY'S Cocoa
1/3 cup powdered sugar
1/3 cup butter or margarine, melted
1 package (10 ounces) frozen raspberries, thawed
1 envelope unflavored gelatin
1/2 cup cold water
1/2 cup boiling water
2 packages (8 ounces each) cream cheese, softened
1/2 cup granulated sugar
1 teaspoon vanilla extract
3 tablespoons seedless red raspberry preserves
Chocolate Whipped Cream (recipe follows)

1. Heat oven to 350°F.

2. Stir together crumbs, cocoa and powdered sugar in medium bowl; stir in melted butter. Press mixture onto bottom and 1 1/2 inches up side of 9-inch springform pan. Bake 10 minutes; cool completely.

3. Purée and strain raspberries; set aside. Sprinkle gelatin over cold water in small bowl; let stand several minutes to soften. Add boiling water; stir until gelatin dissolves completely and mixture is clear. Beat cream cheese, granulated sugar and vanilla in large bowl until smooth. Gradually add raspberry purée and gelatin, mixing thoroughly; pour into prepared crust.

4. Refrigerate several hours or overnight. Loosen cake from side of pan with knife; remove side of pan. Spread raspberry preserves over top. Garnish with Chocolate Whipped Cream. Cover; refrigerate leftovers. *Makes 10 to 12 servings*

Chocolate Whipped Cream: Stir together ½ cup powdered sugar and ¼ cup HERSHEY'S Cocoa in medium bowl. Add ½ pint chilled whipping cream and 1 teaspoon vanilla extract; beat until stiff.

Chilled Raspberry Cheesecake

Orange Streusel Coffeecake

Cocoa Streusel (recipe follows)
$^3/_4$ cup (1$^1/_2$ sticks) butter or margarine, softened
1 cup sugar
3 eggs
1 teaspoon vanilla extract
$^1/_2$ cup dairy sour cream
3 cups all-purpose flour
2 teaspoons baking powder
1 teaspoon baking soda
1 cup orange juice
2 teaspoons grated orange peel
$^1/_2$ cup orange marmalade or apple jelly

1. Prepare Cocoa Streusel. Heat oven to 350°F. Generously grease 12-cup fluted tube pan.

2. Beat butter and sugar in large bowl until well blended. Add eggs and vanilla; beat well. Add sour cream; beat until blended. Stir together flour, baking powder and baking soda; add alternately with orange juice to butter mixture, beating until well blended. Stir in orange peel.

3. Spread marmalade in bottom of prepared pan; sprinkle half of streusel over marmalade. Pour half of batter into pan, spreading evenly. Sprinkle remaining streusel over batter; spread remaining batter evenly over streusel.

4. Bake about 1 hour or until toothpick inserted near center of cake comes out clean. Loosen cake from side of pan with metal spatula; immediately invert onto serving plate. *Makes 12 servings*

Cocoa Streusel: Stir together $^2/_3$ cup packed light brown sugar, $^1/_2$ cup chopped walnuts, $^1/_4$ cup HERSHEY'S Cocoa and $^1/_2$ cup MOUNDS Sweetened Coconut Flakes, if desired.

Orange Streusel Coffeecake

Chocolate Lover's Cheesecake

Graham Crust (recipe follows)
2 packages (8 ounces each) cream cheese, softened
³/₄ cup plus 2 tablespoons sugar, divided
¹/₂ cup HERSHEY'S Cocoa
2 teaspoons vanilla extract, divided
2 eggs
1 cup HERSHEY'S Semi-Sweet Chocolate Chips
1 container (8 ounces) dairy sour cream

1. Prepare Graham Crust. Heat oven to 375°F.

2. Beat cream cheese, ³/₄ cup sugar, cocoa and 1 teaspoon vanilla in large bowl on medium speed of mixer until smooth. Add eggs; beat until blended. Stir in chocolate chips. Pour into prepared crust.

3. Bake 20 minutes. Remove from oven to wire rack; cool 15 minutes. *Increase oven temperature to 425°F.*

4. Stir together sour cream, remaining 2 tablespoons sugar and remaining 1 teaspoon vanilla in small bowl; stir until smooth. Spread over baked filling.

5. Bake 10 minutes. Remove from oven to wire rack. With knife, immediately loosen cake from side of pan. Cool completely; remove side of pan. Refrigerate several hours or until cold. Cover; refrigerate leftover cheesecake. *Makes 10 to 12 servings*

Graham Crust

1¹/₂ cups graham cracker crumbs
¹/₃ cup sugar
¹/₃ cup butter or margarine, melted

Stir together crumbs, sugar and butter in medium bowl. Press mixture onto bottom and halfway up side of 9-inch springform pan.

Chocolate Cheese Pie

1 package (8 ounces) cream cheese, softened
1 package (3 ounces) cream cheese, softened
³/₄ cup sugar
1 teaspoon vanilla extract
¹/₄ cup HERSHEY'S Cocoa
2 eggs
¹/₂ cup whipping cream
1 packaged graham cracker crumb crust (6 ounces)
Cherry pie or peach pie filling or sliced fresh fruit

1. Heat oven to 350°F. Beat cream cheese, sugar and vanilla in large bowl until well blended.

2. Add cocoa; beat until well blended, scraping sides of bowl and beaters frequently. Add eggs; beat well. Stir in whipping cream. Pour into crust.

3. Bake 35 to 40 minutes. (Center will be soft but will set upon cooling.) Cool to room temperature. Cover; refrigerate several hours or overnight. Serve with pie filling. Cover; refrigerate leftover pie.

Makes 6 to 8 servings

Prep Time: 10 minutes
Bake Time: 35 minutes
Chill Time: 4 to 6 hours

Hot Fudge Pudding Cake

1 1/4 cups granulated sugar, divided
  1 cup all-purpose flour
  1/2 cup HERSHEY'S Cocoa, divided
  2 teaspoons baking powder
  1/4 teaspoon salt
  1/2 cup milk
  1/3 cup butter or margarine, melted
1 1/2 teaspoons vanilla extract
  1/2 cup packed light brown sugar
1 1/4 cups hot water
    Whipped topping

1. Heat oven to 350°F.

2. Stir together 3/4 cup granulated sugar, flour, 1/4 cup cocoa, baking powder and salt. Stir in milk, butter and vanilla; beat until smooth. Pour batter into ungreased 9-inch square baking pan. Stir together remaining 1/2 cup granulated sugar, brown sugar and remaining 1/4 cup cocoa; sprinkle mixture evenly over batter. Pour hot water over top. Do not stir.

3. Bake 35 to 40 minutes or until center is almost set. Let stand 15 minutes; spoon into dessert dishes, spooning sauce from bottom of pan over top. Garnish with whipped topping.

Makes about 8 servings

Prep Time: 10 minutes
Bake Time: 35 minutes
Cool Time: 15 minutes

Hot Fudge Pudding Cake

Classic Hershey Bar Cake

1 cup (2 sticks) butter or margarine, softened
1¼ cups granulated sugar
4 eggs
6 HERSHEY'S Milk Chocolate Bars (1.55 ounces each), melted
2½ cups all-purpose flour
¼ teaspoon baking soda
Dash salt
1 cup buttermilk or sour milk*
½ cup HERSHEY'S Syrup
2 teaspoons vanilla extract
1 cup chopped pecans
Powdered sugar (optional)

To sour milk: Use 1 tablespoon white vinegar plus milk to equal 1 cup.

1. Heat oven to 350°F. Grease and flour 10-inch tube pan or 12-cup fluted tube pan.

2. Beat butter in large bowl until creamy; gradually add granulated sugar, beating on medium speed of mixer until well blended. Add eggs, one at a time, beating well after each addition. Add chocolate; beat until blended.

3. Stir together flour, baking soda and salt; add to chocolate mixture alternately with buttermilk, beating until blended. Add syrup and vanilla; beat until blended. Stir in pecans. Pour batter into prepared pan.

4. Bake 1 hour and 15 minutes or until wooden pick inserted in center of cake comes out clean. Cool 10 minutes; remove from pan to wire rack. Cool completely. Sift powdered sugar over top, if desired.

Makes 12 to 16 servings

Chocolate Truffle Cake Supreme

1$\frac{1}{4}$ cups (2$\frac{1}{2}$ sticks) unsalted butter
$\frac{3}{4}$ cup HERSHEY'S Cocoa
1 cup plus 1 tablespoon sugar, divided
1 tablespoon all-purpose flour
2 teaspoons vanilla extract
4 eggs, separated
1 cup ($\frac{1}{2}$ pint) cold whipping cream
Chocolate curls (optional)

1. Heat oven to 425°F. Grease bottom of 8-inch springform pan. Melt butter in medium saucepan over low heat. Add cocoa and 1 cup sugar; stir well. Remove from heat; cool. Stir in flour and vanilla. Add egg yolks, one at a time, beating well after each. Beat egg whites in medium bowl with remaining 1 tablespoon sugar until soft peaks form; gradually fold into chocolate mixture. Spoon batter into pan.

2. Bake 16 to 18 minutes or until edge is firm (center will be soft). Cool completely on wire rack (cake will sink slightly in center as it cools). Remove side of pan. Refrigerate cake at least 6 hours.

3. Beat whipping cream in small bowl until soft peaks form; spread over top of cake. Cut cake while cold, but let stand at room temperature 10 to 15 minutes before serving. Garnish with chocolate curls, if desired. *Makes 10 servings*

Prep Time: 20 minutes
Bake Time: 16 minutes
Cool Time: 1 hour
Chill Time: 6 hours

Hershey's "Perfectly Chocolate" Chocolate Cake

     2 cups sugar
 1 3/4 cups all-purpose flour
     3/4 cup HERSHEY'S Cocoa or HERSHEY'S Dutch Processed
        Cocoa
 1 1/2 teaspoons baking powder
 1 1/2 teaspoons baking soda
     1 teaspoon salt
     2 eggs
     1 cup milk
     1/2 cup vegetable oil
     2 teaspoons vanilla extract
     1 cup boiling water
        "Perfectly Chocolate" Chocolate Frosting (recipe follows)

1. Heat oven to 350°F. Grease and flour two 9-inch round baking pans.*

2. Stir together sugar, flour, cocoa, baking powder, baking soda and salt in large bowl. Add eggs, milk, oil and vanilla; beat on medium speed of mixer 2 minutes. Stir in water. (Batter will be thin.) Pour batter evenly into prepared pans.

3. Bake 30 to 35 minutes or until wooden pick inserted in center comes out clean. Cool 10 minutes; remove from pans to wire racks. Cool completely.

4. Prepare "Perfectly Chocolate" Chocolate Frosting; spread between layers and over top and sides of cake.   *Makes 8 to 10 servings*

One 13×9×2-inch baking pan may be substituted for 9-inch round baking pans. Prepare as directed above. Bake 35 to 40 minutes. Cool completely in pan on wire rack. Frost as desired.

"Perfectly Chocolate" Chocolate Frosting

$^1/_2$ cup (1 stick) butter or margarine
$^2/_3$ cup HERSHEY'S Cocoa
3 cups powdered sugar
$^1/_3$ cup milk
1 teaspoon vanilla extract

1. Melt butter. Stir in cocoa. Alternately add powdered sugar and milk, beating to spreading consistency.

2. Add small amount additional milk, if needed. Stir in vanilla.

Makes about 2 cups frosting

Hershey's "Perfectly Chocolate" Chocolate Cake

Take-Me-To-A-Picnic Cake

   1 cup water
   1 cup (2 sticks) butter or margarine
  $^1/_2$ cup HERSHEY'S Cocoa
   2 cups sugar
1$^3/_4$ cups all-purpose flour
   1 teaspoon baking soda
  $^1/_2$ teaspoon salt
   3 eggs
  $^3/_4$ cup dairy sour cream
     Peanut Butter Chip Frosting (recipe follows)
     Chocolate Garnish (recipe follows, optional)

1. Heat oven to 350°F. Grease and flour 15$^1/_2$×10$^1/_2$×1-inch jelly-roll pan.

2. Combine water, butter and cocoa in medium saucepan. Cook over medium heat, stirring occasionally, until mixture boils. Boil 1 minute. Remove from heat. Stir together sugar, flour, baking soda and salt in large bowl. Add eggs and sour cream; beat until blended. Add cocoa mixture; beat just until blended. Pour into prepared pan.

3. Bake 25 to 30 minutes or until wooden pick inserted in center comes out clean. Cool on wire rack. Prepare Peanut Butter Chip Frosting. Spread over cake. Prepare Chocolate Garnish; drizzle over top, if desired. *Makes about 20 servings*

Peanut Butter Chip Frosting: Combine $^1/_3$ cup butter or margarine, $^1/_3$ cup milk and 1$^2/_3$ cups (10-ounce package) REESE'S Peanut Butter Chips in medium saucepan. Cook over low heat, stirring constantly, until chips are melted and mixture is smooth. Remove from heat; stir in 1 teaspoon vanilla extract. Place 1 cup powdered sugar in medium bowl. Gradually add chip mixture; beat well. Makes about 2 cups frosting.

Chocolate Garnish: Place ½ cup HERSHEY'S Semi-Sweet Chocolate Chips and 1 teaspoon shortening (not butter, margarine, spread or oil) in small microwave-safe bowl. Microwave at HIGH (100%) 1 minute; stir until chips are melted and mixture is smooth.

Prep Time: 30 minutes
Bake Time: 25 minutes
Cool Time: 1 hour

Take-Me-To-A-Picnic Cake

Easy Chocolate Cream-Filled Torte

    1 frozen pound cake (10³/₄ ounces), thawed
    ¹/₂ cup powdered sugar
    ¹/₄ cup HERSHEY'S Cocoa
    1 cup (¹/₂ pint) cold whipping cream
    1 teaspoon vanilla extract
      Chocolate Glaze (recipe follows)
      Sliced almonds (optional)

1. Cut cake horizontally to make 4 layers. Stir together sugar and cocoa in medium bowl. Add whipping cream and vanilla; beat until stiff.

2. Place bottom cake layer on serving platter. Spread ¹/₃ of the whipped cream mixture on cake layer. Place next cake layer on top of whipped cream mixture; continue layering whipped cream mixture and cake until all have been used.

3. Prepare Chocolate Glaze; spoon over top of cake, allowing to drizzle down sides. Garnish with almonds, if desired. Refrigerate until ready to serve. Cover; refrigerate leftover torte.

Makes 8 to 10 servings

Prep Time: 20 minutes
Chill Time: 30 minutes

Chocolate Glaze

    2 tablespoons butter or margarine
    2 tablespoons HERSHEY'S Cocoa
    2 tablespoons water
    1 cup powdered sugar
    ¹/₄ to ¹/₂ teaspoon almond extract

1. Melt butter in small saucepan over low heat. Add cocoa and water. Cook, stirring constantly, until smooth and slightly thickened. Do not boil.

2. Remove from heat. Gradually add powdered sugar and almond extract, beating with whisk until smooth. *Makes about ¹/₂ cup glaze*

Easy Chocolate Cream-Filled Torte

Old-Fashioned Chocolate Cake

$3/4$ cup ($1^1/2$ sticks) butter or margarine, softened
$1^2/3$ cups sugar
3 eggs
1 teaspoon vanilla extract
2 cups all-purpose flour
$2/3$ cup HERSHEY'S Cocoa
$1^1/4$ teaspoons baking soda
1 teaspoon salt
$1/4$ teaspoon baking powder
$1^1/3$ cups water
$1/2$ cup finely crushed hard peppermint candy (optional)
One-Bowl Buttercream Frosting (recipe follows)
Additional crushed hard peppermint candy (optional)

1. Heat oven to 350°F. Grease and flour two 9-inch round baking pans or one 13×9×2-inch baking pan.

2. Combine butter, sugar, eggs and vanilla in large bowl; beat on high speed of mixer 3 minutes. Stir together flour, cocoa, baking soda, salt and baking powder; add alternately with water to butter mixture. Blend just until combined; add candy, if desired. Pour batter into prepared pans.

3. Bake 30 to 35 minutes or until wooden pick inserted in centers comes out clean. Cool 10 minutes; remove from pans to wire racks. Cool completely.

4. Frost with One-Bowl Buttercream Frosting. Just before serving, garnish with peppermint candy, if desired.   *Makes 8 to 10 servings*

One-Bowl Buttercream Frosting

6 tablespoons butter or margarine, softened
2²/₃ cups powdered sugar
¹/₂ cup HERSHEY'S Cocoa or HERSHEY'S Dutch Processed
Cocoa
4 to 6 tablespoons milk
1 teaspoon vanilla extract

Beat butter in medium bowl. Add powdered sugar and cocoa
alternately with milk, beating to spreading consistency. Stir in vanilla.

Makes about 2 cups frosting

Fudge Truffle Cheesecake

        Chocolate Crumb Crust (recipe follows)
    2 cups (12-ounce package) HERSHEY'S Semi-Sweet
        Chocolate Chips
    3 packages (8 ounces each) cream cheese, softened
    1 can (14 ounces) sweetened condensed milk (not evaporated
        milk)
    4 eggs
    2 teaspoons vanilla extract

1. Prepare Chocolate Crumb Crust; set aside. Heat oven to 300°F.

2. Place chocolate chips in microwave-safe bowl. Microwave at HIGH
(100%) 1 1/2 minutes; stir. If necessary, microwave at HIGH an
additional 15 seconds at a time, stirring after each heating, just until
chips are melted when stirred.

3. Beat cream cheese in large bowl until fluffy. Gradually beat in
sweetened condensed milk until smooth. Add melted chips, eggs and
vanilla; mix well. Pour into prepared crust.

4. Bake 1 hour and 5 minutes or until center is set. Remove from
oven to wire rack. With knife, loosen cake from side of pan. Cool
completely; remove side of pan. Refrigerate several hours before
serving. Garnish as desired. Cover; refrigerate leftover cheesecake.
Makes 10 to 12 servings

Chocolate Crumb Crust: Stir together 1 1/2 cups vanilla wafer
crumbs, 1/2 cup powdered sugar, 1/3 cup HERSHEY'S Cocoa and
1/3 cup melted butter or margarine in bowl. Press firmly onto bottom
of 9-inch springform pan.

Tip: Chocolate should be stored in a cool, dry place (60°F to 70°F.)
When chocolate is exposed to varying temperatures, "bloom", a
gray-white film, sometimes appears on the surface. It does not affect
the taste or quality of the chocolate.

Prep Time: 25 minutes
Bake Time: 1 hour 5 minutes
Cool Time: 1 1/2 hours
Chill Time: 4 hours

Fudge Truffle Cheesecake

Our Gal Sundae Pie

Macaroon-Nut Crust (recipe follows)
$^2/_3$ cup packed light brown sugar
3 tablespoons all-purpose flour
2 tablespoons cornstarch
$^1/_2$ teaspoon salt
$2^1/_4$ cups milk
$^1/_2$ cup HERSHEY'S Syrup
3 egg yolks, well beaten
2 tablespoons butter (do not use margarine)
1 teaspoon vanilla extract
Sweetened whipped cream (optional)
Maraschino cherries (optional)
1 HERSHEY'S Milk Chocolate Bar (1.55 ounces), broken into pieces (optional)

1. Prepare Macaroon-Nut Crust.

2. Stir together brown sugar, flour, cornstarch and salt in medium saucepan. Gradually stir in milk, syrup and egg yolks until blended. Cook over medium heat, stirring constantly, until mixture comes to a boil; boil 1 minute, stirring constantly. Remove from heat; stir in butter and vanilla. Pour mixture into prepared crust. Press plastic wrap directly onto surface. Cool on wire rack; refrigerate at least 6 hours.

3. Just before serving, garnish with sweetened whipped cream, maraschino cherries and chocolate bar pieces, if desired. Cover; refrigerate leftover pie. *Makes 8 servings*

Macaroon-Nut Crust

1 $\frac{1}{4}$ cups coconut macaroon cookie crumbs (use purchased hard
   coconut macaroon cookies)
$\frac{1}{2}$ cup chopped walnuts
$\frac{1}{4}$ cup ($\frac{1}{2}$ stick) butter (do not use margarine), melted

1. Heat oven to 350°F.

2. Stir together cookie crumbs, walnuts and butter in medium bowl. Press firmly onto bottom and up side of 9-inch pie plate.

3. Bake 8 to 10 minutes or until lightly browned. Cool completely.

Chocolate Raspberry Pound Cake

      1 cup seedless black raspberry preserves, divided*
      2 cups all-purpose flour
 1 1/2 cups granulated sugar
      3/4 cup HERSHEY'S Cocoa
 1 1/2 teaspoons baking soda
      1 teaspoon salt
      2/3 cup butter or margarine, softened
      1 container (16 ounces) dairy sour cream
      2 eggs
      1 teaspoon vanilla extract
        Powdered sugar
        Raspberry Cream (recipe follows)

Red raspberry preserves can be substituted.

1. Heat oven to 350°F. Grease and flour 12-cup fluted tube pan.

2. Place 3/4 cup preserves in small microwave-safe bowl. Microwave at HIGH (100%) 30 to 45 seconds or until melted; cool. Stir together flour, granulated sugar, cocoa, baking soda and salt in large bowl. Add butter, sour cream, eggs, vanilla and melted preserves; beat on medium speed of mixer 3 to 4 minutes until well blended. Pour batter into prepared pan.

3. Bake 50 to 60 minutes or until wooden pick inserted in center comes out clean. Cool 10 minutes; remove from pan to wire rack. Place remaining 1/4 cup preserves in small microwave-safe bowl. Microwave at HIGH 30 seconds or until melted; brush over warm cake. Cool completely.

4. At serving time, sprinkle powdered sugar over top. Prepare Raspberry Cream; fill cavity with cream. Garnish, if desired.

Makes about 12 servings

Raspberry Cream: Thaw 1 package (10 ounces) frozen red raspberries in light syrup. Purée in food processor or blender. Strain into medium bowl; discard seeds. Blend 1 tub (8 ounces) frozen non-dairy whipped topping, thawed, with raspberry purée. Stir in 2 tablespoons raspberry-flavored liqueur, if desired.

Prep Time: 35 minutes
Bake Time: 50 minutes
Cool Time: 3 hours

Chocolate Raspberry Pound Cake

Decadent Desserts

When you want to impress your guests, all it takes is a fabulous chocolate dessert. Try a mousse, soufflé, cream puffs or crêpes—the hardest part is deciding what to make!

Two Great Tastes Pudding Parfaits

    1 package (6-serving size, 4.6 ounces) vanilla cook & serve
       pudding and pie filling mix*
3¹/₂ cups milk
    1 cup REESE'S Peanut Butter Chips
    1 cup HERSHEY'S MINI KISSES™ Semi-Sweet or Milk
       Chocolates
      Whipped topping (optional)
      Additional MINI KISSES™ Chocolates or grated chocolate

*Do not use instant pudding mix.

1. Combine pudding mix and 3¹/₂ cups milk in large heavy saucepan
(rather than amount listed in package directions). Cook over medium
heat, stirring constantly, until mixture comes to a full boil. Remove
from heat; divide hot mixture between 2 heat-proof medium bowls.

2. Immediately stir peanut butter chips into mixture in one bowl and
Mini Kisses™ Chocolates into second bowl. Stir both mixtures until
chips are melted and mixture is smooth. Cool slightly, stirring
occasionally.

3. Alternately layer peanut butter and chocolate mixtures in parfait
dishes, wine glasses or dessert dishes. Place plastic wrap directly onto
surface of each dessert; refrigerate about 6 hours. Garnish with
whipped topping, if desired, and Mini Kisses™ Chocolates.

Makes 4 to 6 servings

69

Napoleons

> 1 package (17¼ ounces) frozen puff pastry sheets
> Chocolate Filling (recipe follows)
> Vanilla Glaze (recipe follows)
> Chocolate Glaze (recipe follows)

1. Thaw folded pastry sheets as package directs. Heat oven to 350°F. Gently unfold sheets. On lightly floured surface, roll each sheet to 15×12-inch rectangle; trim to even edges. Place on large ungreased baking sheets; prick each sheet thoroughly with fork. Bake 18 to 20 minutes or until puffed and golden brown. Cool completely on baking sheets.

2. Prepare Chocolate Filling.

3. Cut one rectangle lengthwise into 3 equal pieces. Place one piece on serving plate; spread with one fourth of the Chocolate Filling. Top with second piece of pastry; spread with one fourth of the filling. Place remaining piece on top; set aside. Repeat with remaining pastry and filling.

4. Prepare Vanilla Glaze; spread onto top of each pastry. Prepare Chocolate Glaze; drizzle over Vanilla Glaze in decorative design. Refrigerate at least 1 hour or until filling is set. Carefully cut each pastry into 6 pieces. Cover; refrigerate leftovers.

Makes 12 servings

Chocolate Filling

> 1 envelope unflavored gelatin
> 2 tablespoons cold water
> ¼ cup boiling water
> 1 cup sugar
> ½ cup HERSHEY'S Cocoa
> 2 cups (1 pint) cold whipping cream
> 2 teaspoons vanilla extract

1. Sprinkle gelatin over cold water in small bowl; let stand 1 minute to soften. Add boiling water; stir until gelatin is completely dissolved and mixture is clear. Cool slightly.

2. Stir together sugar and cocoa in large bowl. Add whipping cream and vanilla; beat at medium speed of mixer, scraping bottom of bowl occasionally, until stiff. Add gelatin mixture; beat until well blended. Refrigerate to spreading consistency, if necessary.

Makes about 5 cups

Vanilla Glaze: Combine 1 1/2 cups powdered sugar, 1 tablespoon light corn syrup, 1/4 teaspoon vanilla extract and 1 to 2 tablespoons hot water in small bowl; beat to spreading consistency. (Add additional water, 1/2 teaspoon at a time, if necessary.)

Chocolate Glaze: Melt 1/4 cup butter or margarine in small saucepan. Remove from heat; stir in 1/3 cup HERSHEY'S Cocoa until smooth. Cool slightly.

Cocoa Cappuccino Mousse

1 can (14 ounces) sweetened condensed milk (not evaporated milk)
1/3 cup HERSHEY'S Cocoa
3 tablespoons butter or margarine
2 teaspoons powdered instant coffee or espresso, dissolved in 2 teaspoons hot water
2 cups (1 pint) cold whipping cream

1. Combine sweetened condensed milk, cocoa, butter and coffee in medium saucepan. Cook over low heat, stirring constantly, until butter melts and mixture is smooth. Remove from heat; cool.

2. Beat whipping cream in large bowl until stiff. Gradually fold chocolate mixture into whipped cream. Spoon into dessert dishes. Refrigerate until set, about 2 hours. Garnish as desired.

Makes 8 servings

Prep Time: 15 minutes
Cook Time: 10 minutes
Chill Time: 2 hours

Cocoa Cappuccino Mousse

Hot Chocolate Soufflé

    ³/₄ cup HERSHEY'S Cocoa
     1 cup sugar, divided
    ¹/₂ cup all-purpose flour
    ¹/₄ teaspoon salt
     2 cups milk
     6 egg yolks, well beaten
     2 tablespoons butter or margarine
     1 teaspoon vanilla extract
     8 egg whites
    ¹/₄ teaspoon cream of tartar
       Sweetened whipped cream

1. Adjust oven rack to lowest position. Heat oven to 350°F. Lightly butter 2¹/₂-quart soufflé dish; sprinkle with sugar. For collar, cut a length of heavy-duty aluminum foil to fit around soufflé dish; fold in thirds lengthwise. Lightly butter one side of foil. Attach foil, buttered side in, around outside of dish, allowing foil to extend at least 2 inches above dish. Secure foil with tape or string.

2. Stir together cocoa, ³/₄ cup sugar, flour and salt in large saucepan; gradually stir in milk. Cook over medium heat, stirring constantly with wire whisk, until mixture boils; remove from heat. Gradually stir small amount of chocolate mixture into beaten egg yolks; blend well. Add egg mixture to chocolate mixture in pan, blending well. Cook and stir 1 minute. Add butter and vanilla, stirring until blended. Set aside; cool 20 minutes.

3. Beat egg whites with cream of tartar in large bowl until soft peaks form; gradually add remaining ¹/₄ cup sugar, beating until stiff peaks form. Gently fold about one-third of beaten egg white mixture into chocolate mixture. Lightly fold chocolate mixture, half at a time, into remaining beaten egg white mixture just until blended; do not overfold.

4. Gently pour mixture into prepared dish; smooth top with spatula. Gently place dish in larger baking pan; pour hot water into larger pan to depth of 1 inch.

5. Bake 65 to 70 minutes or until puffed and set. Remove soufflé dish from water. Carefully remove foil. Serve immediately with sweetened whipped cream. *Makes 8 to 10 servings*

Hot Chocolate Soufflé

Cocoa Black Forest Crêpes

3 eggs
3/4 cup water
1/2 cup light cream or half-and-half
3/4 cup plus 2 tablespoons all-purpose flour
3 tablespoons HERSHEY'S Cocoa
2 tablespoons sugar
1/8 teaspoon salt
3 tablespoons butter or margarine, melted and cooled
Cherry pie filling
Chocolate Sauce (recipe follows)
Sweetened whipped cream (optional)

1. Combine eggs, water and light cream in blender or food processor; blend 10 seconds. Add flour, cocoa, sugar, salt and butter; blend until smooth. Let stand at room temperature 30 minutes.

2. Spray 6-inch crêpe pan lightly with vegetable cooking spray; heat over medium heat. For each crêpe, pour 2 to 3 tablespoons batter into pan; lift and tilt pan to spread batter. Return to heat; cook until surface begins to dry. Loosen crêpe around edge; turn and lightly cook other side. Stack crêpes, placing wax paper between crêpes. Keep covered. (Refrigerate for later use, if desired.)

3. Just before serving, place 2 tablespoons pie filling onto each crêpe; roll up. Place crêpes on dessert plate. Prepare Chocolate Sauce; spoon over crêpes. Garnish with sweetened whipped cream, if desired.

Makes about 18 crêpes

Chocolate Sauce: Stir together 3/4 cup sugar and 1/3 cup HERSHEY'S Cocoa in small saucepan; add in 1/2 cup plus 2 tablespoons (5-ounce can) evaporated milk, 1/4 cup (1/2 stick) butter or margarine and 1/8 teaspoon salt. Cook over medium heat, stirring constantly, until mixture comes to a boil. Remove from heat; stir in 1 teaspoon kirsch (cherry brandy), if desired. Serve warm. Cover; refrigerate leftover sauce. Makes about 1 1/2 cups sauce.

Luscious Cocoa Smoothies

　　¼ cup HERSHEY'S Cocoa
　　2 tablespoons sugar
　　3 tablespoons warm water
　　1 banana, peeled and sliced
1½ cups nonfat milk
　　2 cups nonfat frozen yogurt

Stir together cocoa and sugar in small bowl. Add water; stir until well blended. Place banana and cocoa mixture in blender container. Cover; blend until smooth. Add milk and frozen yogurt. Cover; blend until smooth. Serve immediately. *Makes 4 servings*

Royal Hot Chocolate

　　2 bars (1 ounce each) HERSHEY'S Unsweetened Baking
　　　　Chocolate, broken into pieces
　　1 can (14 ounces) sweetened condensed milk (not evaporated
　　　　milk)
　　4 cups boiling water
　　1 teaspoon vanilla extract
　　　Dash salt
　　　Sweetened whipped cream (optional)
　　　Ground cinnamon (optional)

Melt chocolate in large heavy saucepan over low heat. Stir in sweetened condensed milk. Gradually add water, stirring until well blended. Stir in vanilla and salt. Garnish with whipped cream and cinnamon, if desired. Serve immediately. *Makes 8 servings*

Mini Chocolate Pies

1 package (4-serving size) vanilla cook & serve pudding and
   pie filling mix*
1 cup HERSHEY'S MINI CHIPS™ Semi-Sweet Chocolate
   Chips
1 package (4 ounces) single serve graham cracker crusts
   (6 crusts)
   Whipped topping
   Additional MINI CHIPS™ Semi-Sweet Chocolate Chips

*Do not use instant pudding mix.

1. Prepare pudding and pie filling mix as directed on package; remove
from heat. Immediately add 1 cup small chocolate chips; stir until
melted. Cool 5 minutes, stirring occasionally.

2. Pour filling into crusts; press plastic wrap directly onto surface.
Refrigerate several hours or until firm. Garnish with whipped topping
and small chocolate chips.   *Makes 6 servings*

Prep Time: 5 minutes
Cook Time: 10 minutes
Cool Time: 5 minutes
Chill Time: 2 hours

Mini Chocolate Pies

Chocolate-Filled Cream Puffs

Chocolate Cream Filling (recipe follows)
1 cup water
$^{1}/_{2}$ cup (1 stick) butter or margarine
$^{1}/_{4}$ teaspoon salt
1 cup all-purpose flour
4 eggs
Chocolate Glaze (recipe follows)

1. Heat oven to 400°F.

2. Bring water, butter and salt to a rolling boil in medium saucepan. Add flour all at once; stir vigorously over low heat about 1 minute or until mixture leaves side of pan and forms a ball. Remove from heat; add eggs, one at a time, beating well after each addition until smooth and velvety.

3. Drop dough by scant $^{1}/_{4}$ cupfuls onto ungreased cookie sheet. Bake 35 to 40 minutes or until puffed and golden brown. While still warm, horizontally slice off small portion of tops; reserve. Remove any soft dough inside; cool completely on wire rack. Prepare and fill puffs with Chocolate Cream Filling. Replace top.

4. Prepare Chocolate Glaze; drizzle over tops of puffs or sprinkle with powdered sugar, if desired. Refrigerate until serving time. Cover, refrigerate leftover puffs.   *Makes about 12 cream puffs*

Chocolate Glaze: Place $^{1}/_{2}$ cup HERSHEY'S Semi-Sweet Chocolate Chips and 1 tablespoon shortening (do not use butter, margarine, spread or oil) in small microwave-safe bowl. Microwave at HIGH (100%) 30 seconds; stir. If necessary, microwave at HIGH an additional 15 seconds at a time, stirring after each heating, just until chips are melted when stirred.

Miniature Cream Puffs: Prepare cream puff dough as directed above. Drop batter by level teaspoons onto ungreased cookie sheet. Bake 15 minutes. Fill as directed above. Makes about 8 dozen miniature cream puffs.

Chocolate Cream Filling

1 1/4 cups granulated sugar
1/3 cup HERSHEY'S Cocoa
1/3 cup cornstarch
1/4 teaspoon salt
3 cups milk
3 egg yolks, slightly beaten
2 tablespoons butter or margarine
1 1/2 teaspoons vanilla extract

Combine granulated sugar, cocoa, cornstarch and salt in medium saucepan; stir in milk. Cook over medium heat, stirring constantly, until mixture boils; boil and stir 1 minute. Remove from heat. Gradually stir small amount of chocolate mixture into egg yolks; blend well. Return egg mixture to chocolate mixture in pan; stir and heat just until boiling. Remove from heat; blend in butter and vanilla. Pour into bowl; press plastic wrap directly onto surface. Refrigerate 1 to 2 hours or until cold.   *Makes about 3 cups filling*

Creamy Double Decker Fudge

1 cup REESE'S Peanut Butter Chips
1 can (14 ounces) sweetened condensed milk (not evaporated
    milk), divided
1 teaspoon vanilla extract, divided
1 cup HERSHEY'S Semi-Sweet Chocolate Chips

1. Line 8-inch square pan with foil.

2. Place peanut butter chips and $2/3$ cup sweetened condensed
milk in small microwave-safe bowl. Microwave at HIGH (100%)
1 to $1^1/2$ minutes, stirring after 1 minute, until chips are melted and
mixture is smooth when stirred. Stir in $1/2$ teaspoon vanilla; spread
evenly into prepared pan.

3. Place remaining sweetened condensed milk and chocolate chips in
another small microwave-safe bowl; repeat above microwave
procedure. Stir in remaining $1/2$ teaspoon vanilla; spread evenly over
peanut butter layer.

4. Cover; refrigerate until firm. Remove from pan; place on cutting
board. Peel off foil. Cut into squares. Store tightly covered in
refrigerator. *Makes about 4 dozen pieces or $1^1/2$ pounds*

Note: For best results, do not double this recipe.

Prep Time: 15 minutes
Cook Time: 3 minutes
Chill Time: 2 hours

Creamy Double Decker Fudge

Butter Almond Crunch

1½ cups HERSHEY'S Semi-Sweet Chocolate Chips or
   HERSHEY'S MINI CHIPS™ Semi-Sweet Chocolate
   Chips, divided
1¾ cups chopped almonds, divided
1½ cups (3 sticks) butter or margarine
1¾ cups sugar
   3 tablespoons light corn syrup
   3 tablespoons water

1. Heat oven to 350°F. Line 13×9×2-inch pan with foil; butter foil.

2. Sprinkle 1 cup chocolate chips into pan; set aside. Spread chopped almonds in shallow baking dish. Bake about 7 minutes or until golden brown, stirring occasionally; set aside.

3. Melt butter in heavy 3-quart saucepan; stir in sugar, corn syrup and water. Cook over medium heat, stirring constantly, to 280°F on a candy thermometer or until mixture separates into hard, brittle threads when dropped into small amount of very cold water. (Bulb of candy thermometer should not rest on bottom of saucepan.)

4. Remove from heat; stir in 1½ cups toasted almonds. Immediately spread mixture evenly over chocolate chips in prepared pan; do not disturb chips. Sprinkle with remaining ¼ cup toasted almonds and remaining ½ cup chocolate chips; cool slightly.

5. Cool completely; remove from pan. Remove foil; break candy into small pieces. Store in airtight container in cool, dry place.

Makes about 2 pounds candy

Butter Almond Crunch

Double Chocolate Truffles

$^1/_2$ cup whipping cream
1 tablespoon butter or margarine
4 bars (1 ounce each) HERSHEY'S Semi-Sweet Baking
   Chocolate, broken into pieces
1 HERSHEY'S Milk Chocolate Bar (7 ounces), broken into
   pieces
1 tablespoon amaretto (almond-flavored liqueur) *or* $^1/_4$ to
   $^1/_2$ teaspoon almond extract
Ground almonds

1. Combine whipping cream and butter in small saucepan. Cook over medium heat, stirring constantly, just until mixture is very hot. Do not boil. Remove from heat; add chocolate, chocolate bar pieces and liqueur. Stir with whisk until smooth.

2. Press plastic wrap directly onto surface; cool several hours or until mixture is firm enough to handle. Shape into 1-inch balls; roll in almonds to coat. Refrigerate until firm, about 2 hours. Store in tightly covered container in refrigerator.   *Makes about 2 dozen candies*

Quick Creamy Chocolate Pudding

$^2/_3$ cup sugar
$^1/_4$ cup HERSHEY'S Cocoa
3 tablespoons cornstarch
$^1/_4$ teaspoon salt
$2^1/_4$ cups milk
2 tablespoons butter or margarine
1 teaspoon vanilla extract
Whipped topping (optional)
Chopped nuts (optional)

1. Stir together sugar, cocoa, cornstarch and salt in medium saucepan; gradually stir in milk. Cook over medium heat, stirring constantly, until mixture boils; boil and stir 1 minute. Remove from heat; stir in butter and vanilla.

2. Pour into individual dessert dishes. Press plastic wrap directly onto surface; refrigerate. Remove plastic wrap. Garnish with whipped topping, if desired.   *Makes 4 to 5 servings*

Microwave Directions: Stir together sugar, cocoa, cornstarch and salt in large microwave-safe bowl; gradually stir in milk. Microwave at HIGH (100%) 7 to 10 minutes or until mixture comes to a full boil, stirring every 2 minutes. Stir in butter and vanilla. Proceed as directed above.

Cashew Macadamia Crunch

2 cups (11.5 ounce package) HERSHEY'S Milk Chocolate Chips
3/4 cup coarsely chopped salted or unsalted cashews
3/4 cup coarsely chopped salted or unsalted macadamia nuts
1/2 cup (1 stick) butter, softened
1/2 cup sugar
2 tablespoons light corn syrup

1. Line 9-inch square pan with foil, extending foil over edges of pan. Butter foil. Cover bottom of prepared pan with chocolate chips.

2. Combine cashews, macadamia nuts, butter, sugar and corn syrup in large heavy skillet; cook over low heat, stirring constantly, until butter is melted and sugar is dissolved. Increase heat to medium; cook, stirring constantly, until mixture begins to cling together and turns medium golden brown (about 10 minutes).

3. Pour mixture over chocolate chips in pan, spreading evenly. Cool. Refrigerate until chocolate is firm. Remove from pan; peel off foil. Break into pieces. Store tightly covered in cool, dry place.

Makes about 1 1/2 pounds

Prep Time: 30 minutes
Cook Time: 10 minutes
Cool Time: 40 minutes
Chill Time: 3 hours

Cashew Macadamia Crunch

Chocolate Coconut Balls

3 bars (1 ounce each) HERSHEY'S Unsweetened Baking
   Chocolate
$^1/_4$ cup ($^1/_2$ stick) butter
$^1/_2$ cup sweetened condensed milk (not evaporated milk)
$^3/_4$ cup granulated sugar
$^1/_4$ cup water
1 tablespoon light corn syrup
1 teaspoon vanilla extract
2 cups MOUNDS Sweetened Coconut Flakes
1 cup chopped nuts
   Powdered sugar

1. Melt chocolate and butter in large heavy saucepan over very low heat. Add sweetened condensed milk; stir to blend. Remove from heat.

2. Stir together granulated sugar, water and corn syrup in small saucepan. Cook over medium heat, stirring constantly, until sugar is dissolved. Cook, without stirring, until mixture reaches 250°F on candy thermometer or until a small amount of syrup, when dropped into very cold water, forms a firm ball which does not flatten when removed from water. (Bulb of candy thermometer should not rest on bottom of saucepan.) Remove from heat; stir into chocolate mixture. Add vanilla, coconut and nuts; stir until well blended.

3. Refrigerate about 30 minutes or until firm enough to handle. Shape into 1-inch balls; roll in powdered sugar. Store tightly covered in cool, dry place.   *Makes about 4 dozen candies*

Note: For best results, do not double this recipe.

Prep Time: 25 minutes
Cook Time: 20 minutes
Chill Time: 30 minutes

Strawberry Chocolate Chip Shortcake

1 cup sugar, divided
$^{1}/_{2}$ cup (1 stick) butter or margarine, softened
1 egg
2 teaspoons vanilla extract, divided
1$^{1}/_{2}$ cups all-purpose flour
$^{1}/_{2}$ teaspoon baking powder
1 cup HERSHEY'S MINI CHIPS™ Semi-Sweet Chocolate
    or HERSHEY'S Semi-Sweet Chocolate Chips, divided
1 container (16 ounces) dairy sour cream
2 eggs
2 cups frozen non-dairy whipped topping, thawed
    Fresh strawberries, rinsed and halved

1. Heat oven to 350°F. Grease 9-inch springform pan.

2. Beat $^{1}/_{2}$ cup sugar and butter in large bowl. Add 1 egg and 1 teaspoon vanilla; beat until creamy. Gradually add flour and baking powder, beating until smooth; stir in $^{1}/_{2}$ cup small chocolate chips. Press mixture onto bottom of prepared pan.

3. Stir together sour cream, remaining $^{1}/_{2}$ cup sugar, 2 eggs and remaining 1 teaspoon vanilla in medium bowl; stir in remaining $^{1}/_{2}$ cup small chocolate chips. Pour over mixture in pan.

4. Bake 50 to 55 minutes until almost set in center and edges are lightly browned. Cool completely on wire rack; remove side of pan. Spread whipped topping over top. Cover; refrigerate. Just before serving, arrange strawberry halves on top of cake; garnish as desired. Refrigerate leftover dessert. *Makes 12 servings*

INDEX

NOTES

_____

_____

_____

_____

_____

_____

_____

_____

_____

_____

_____

_____

_____

_____

_____